FARM ANIMALS
HOW TO DRAW

THIS BOOK BELONGS TO

____

____

____

HOW TO DRAW FARM ANIMALS

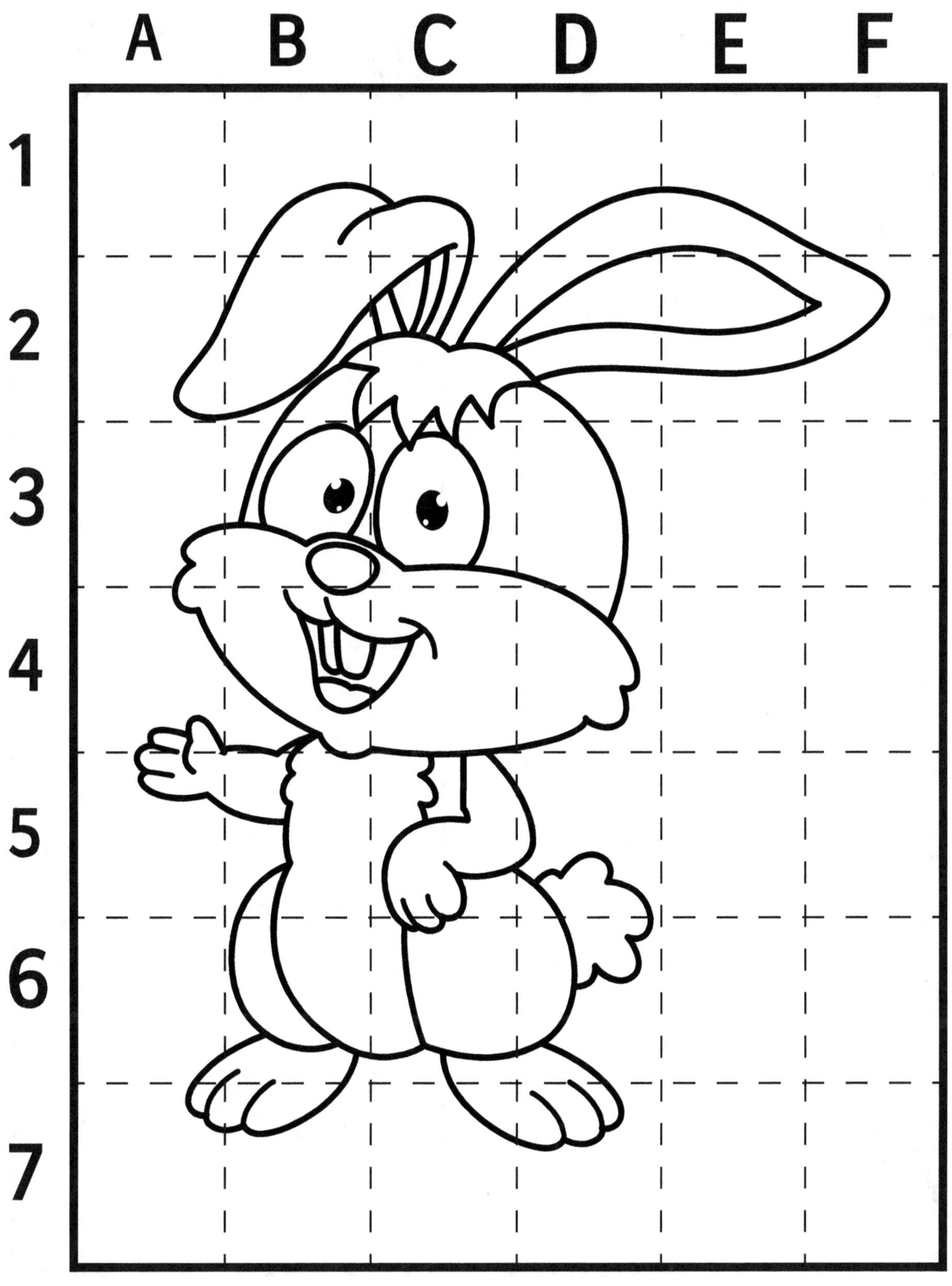

YOUR TURN!

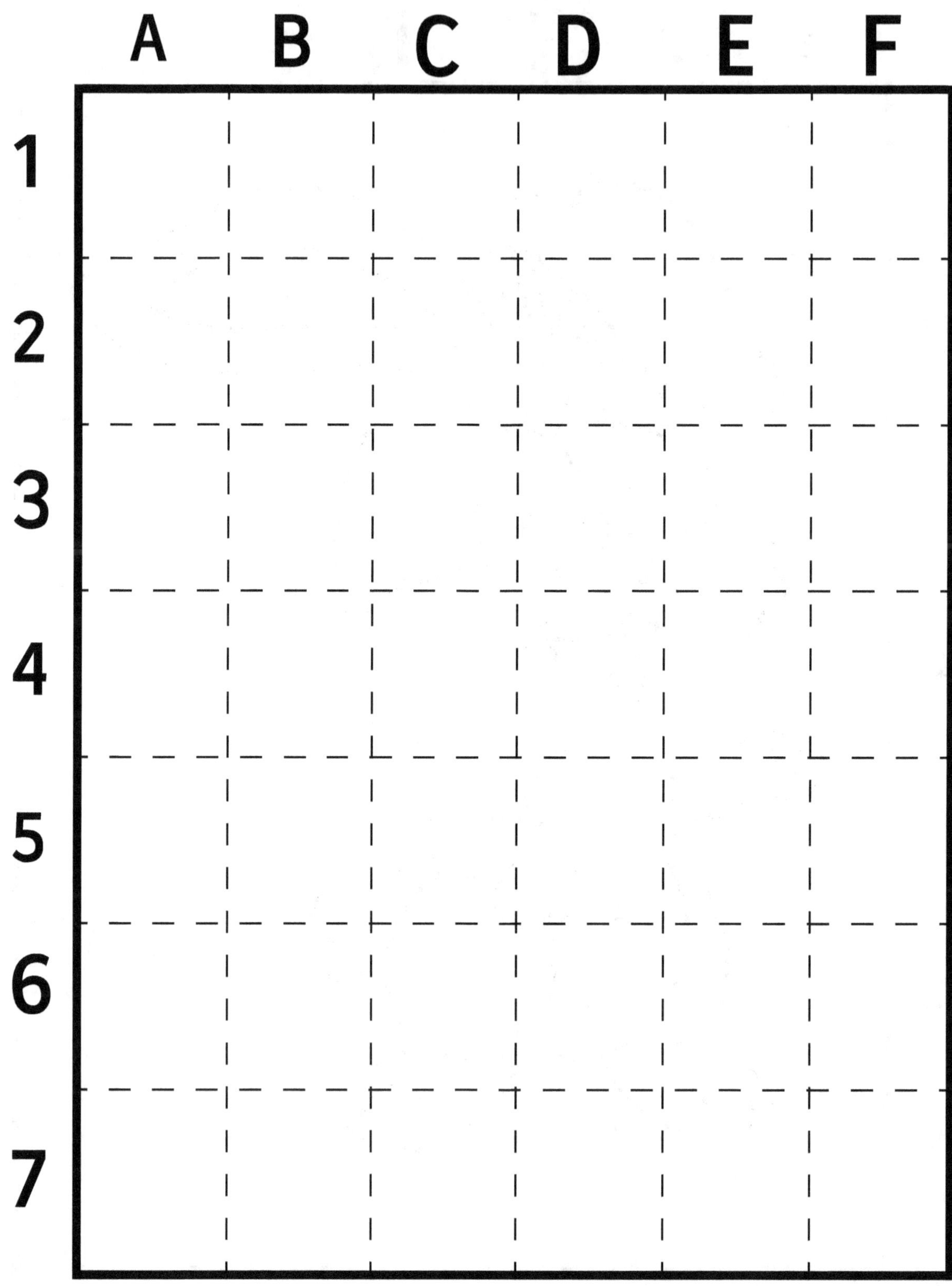

TRACE IT!

MAKE PARFACT

HOW TO DRAW FARM ANIMALS

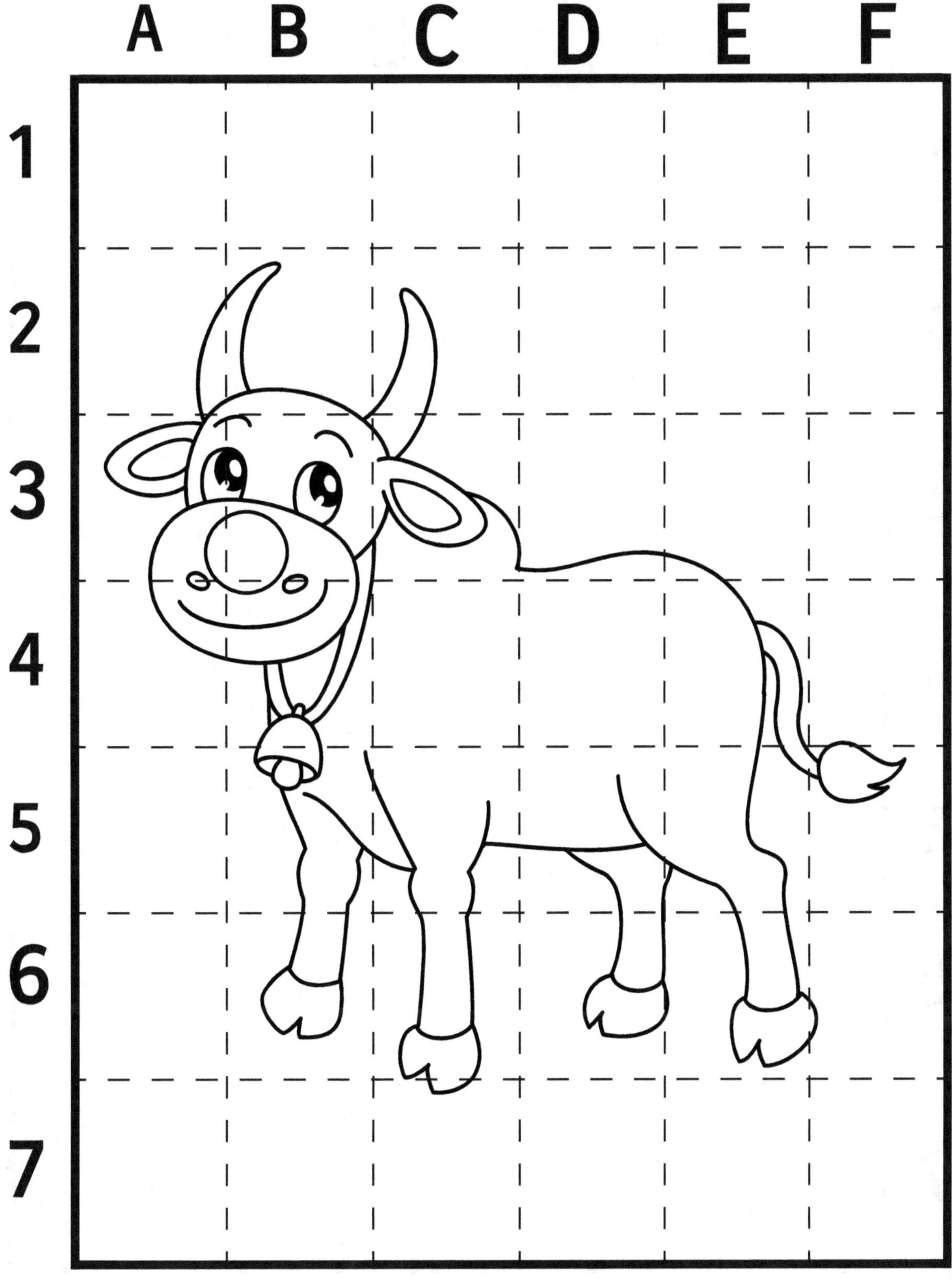

YOUR TURN!

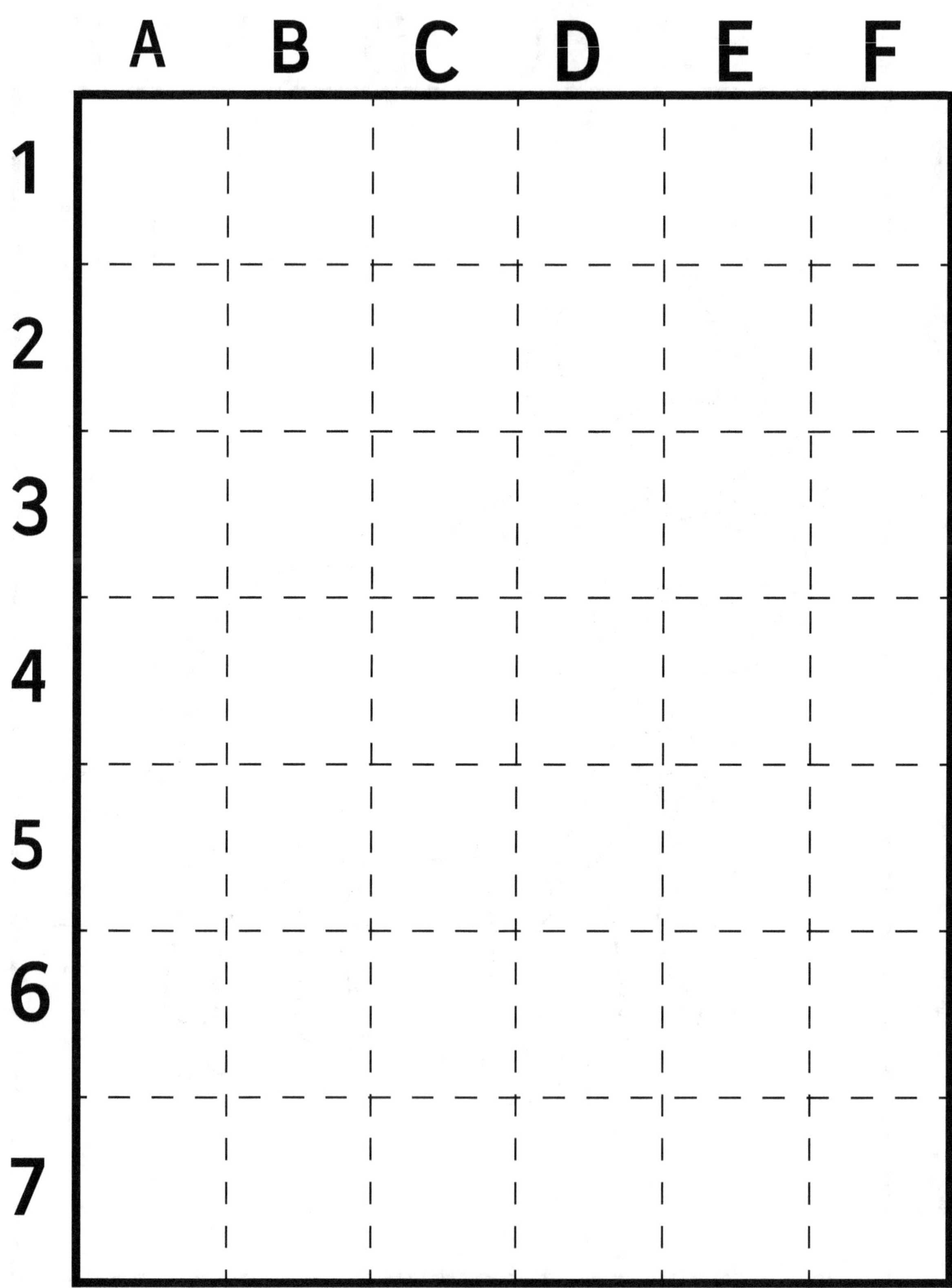

TRACE IT!

MAKE PARFACT

HOW TO DRAW FARM ANIMALS

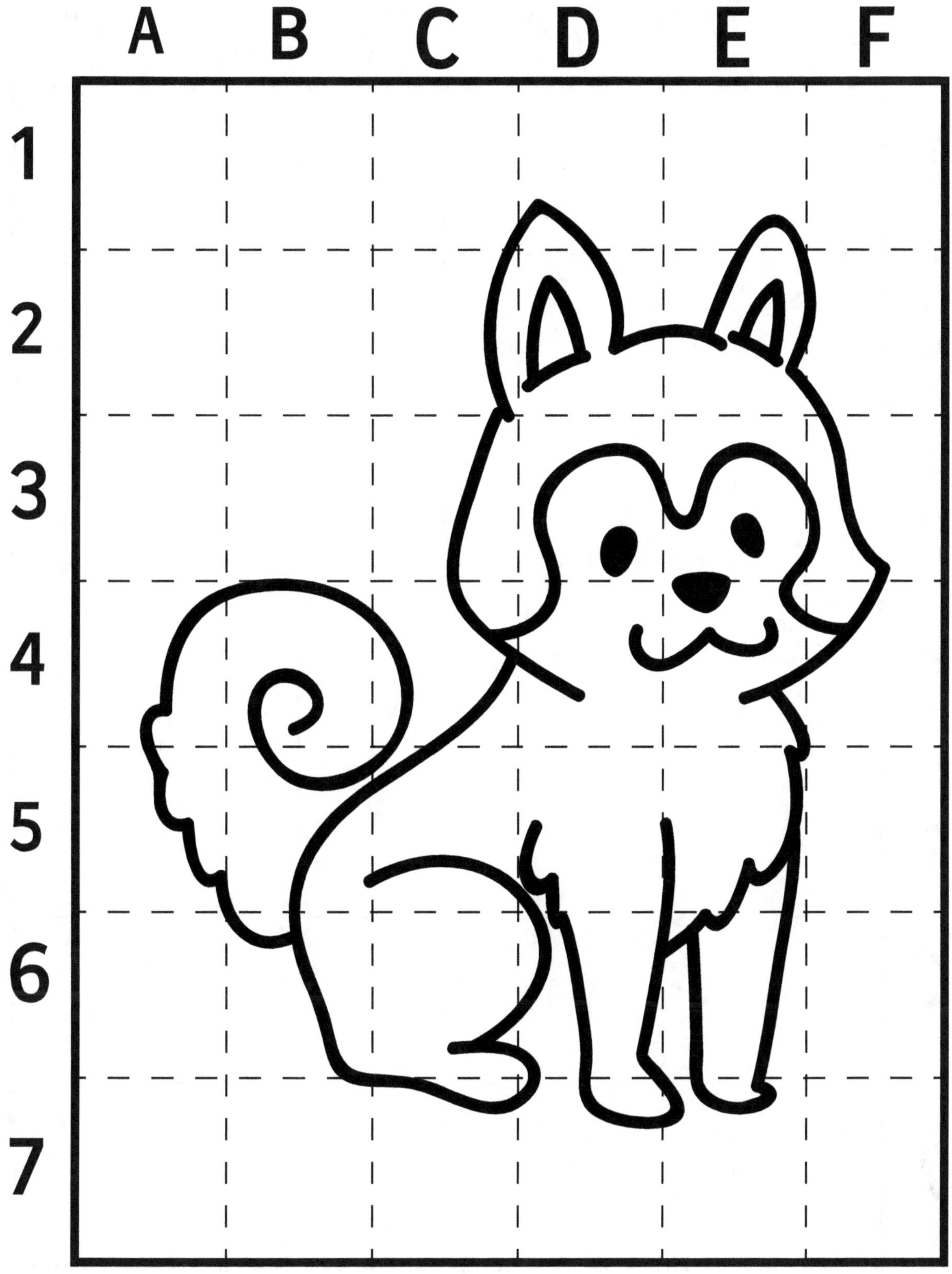

YOUR TURN!

	A	B	C	D	E	F
1						
2						
3						
4						
5						
6						
7						

TRACE IT!

MAKE PARFACT

HOW TO DRAW FARM ANIMALS

A B C D E F

YOUR TURN!

	A	B	C	D	E	F
1						
2						
3						
4						
5						
6						
7						

TRACE IT!

MAKE PARFACT

HOW TO DRAW FARM ANIMALS

A B C D E F

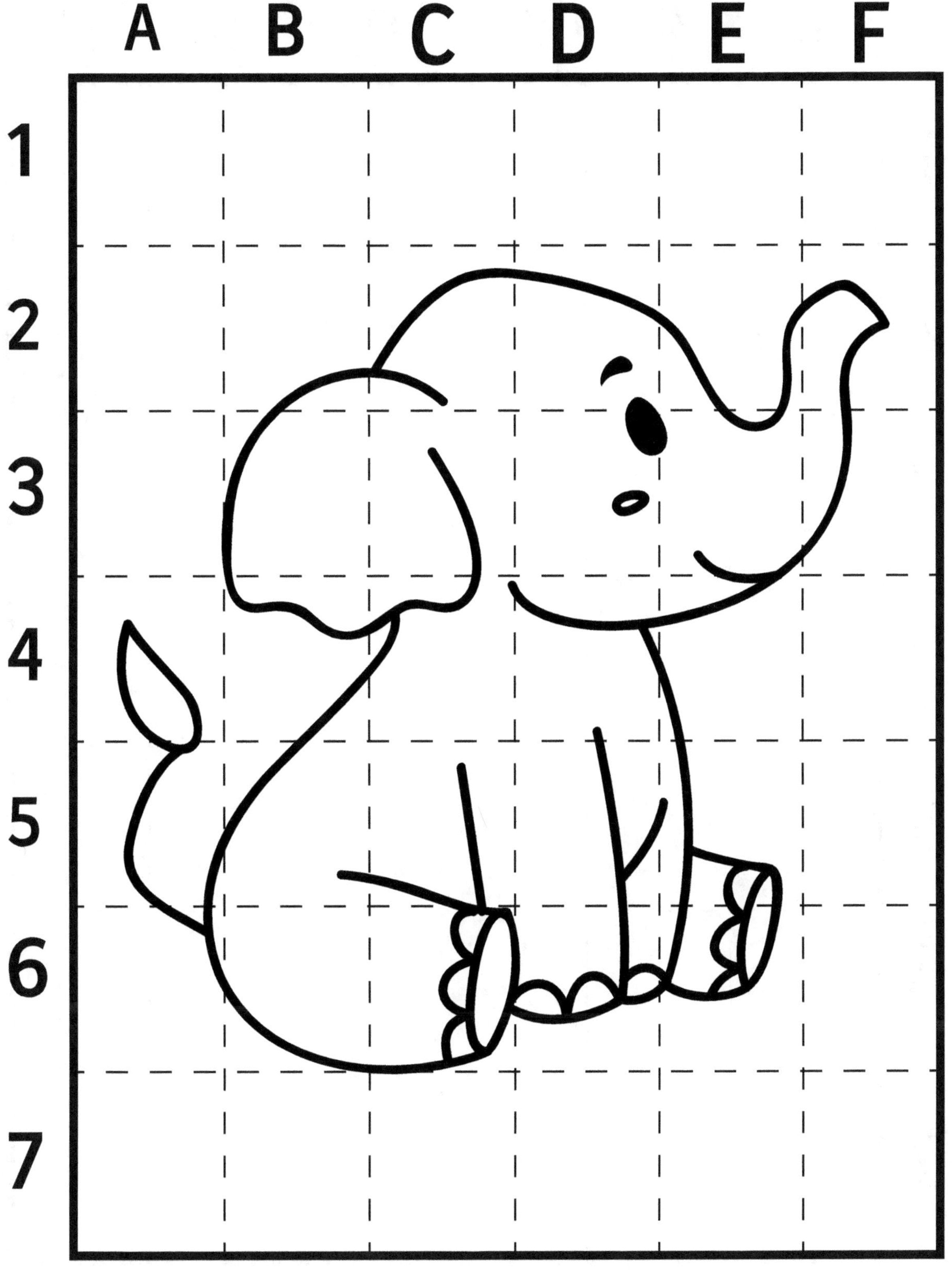

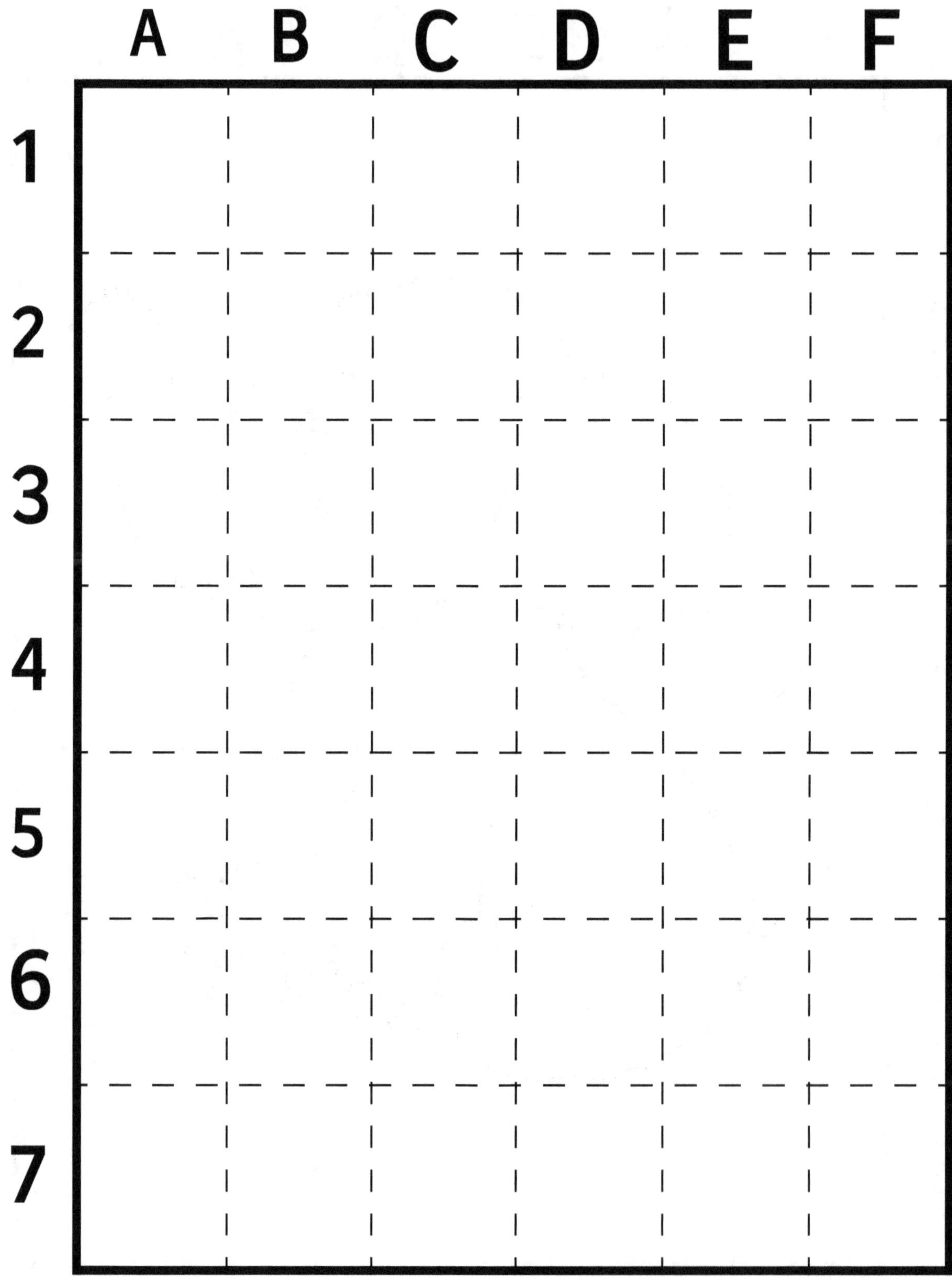

YOUR TURN!
A B C D E F
1
2
3
4
5
6
7

TRACE IT!

MAKE PARFACT

MAKE PARFACT

HOW TO DRAW FARM ANIMALS

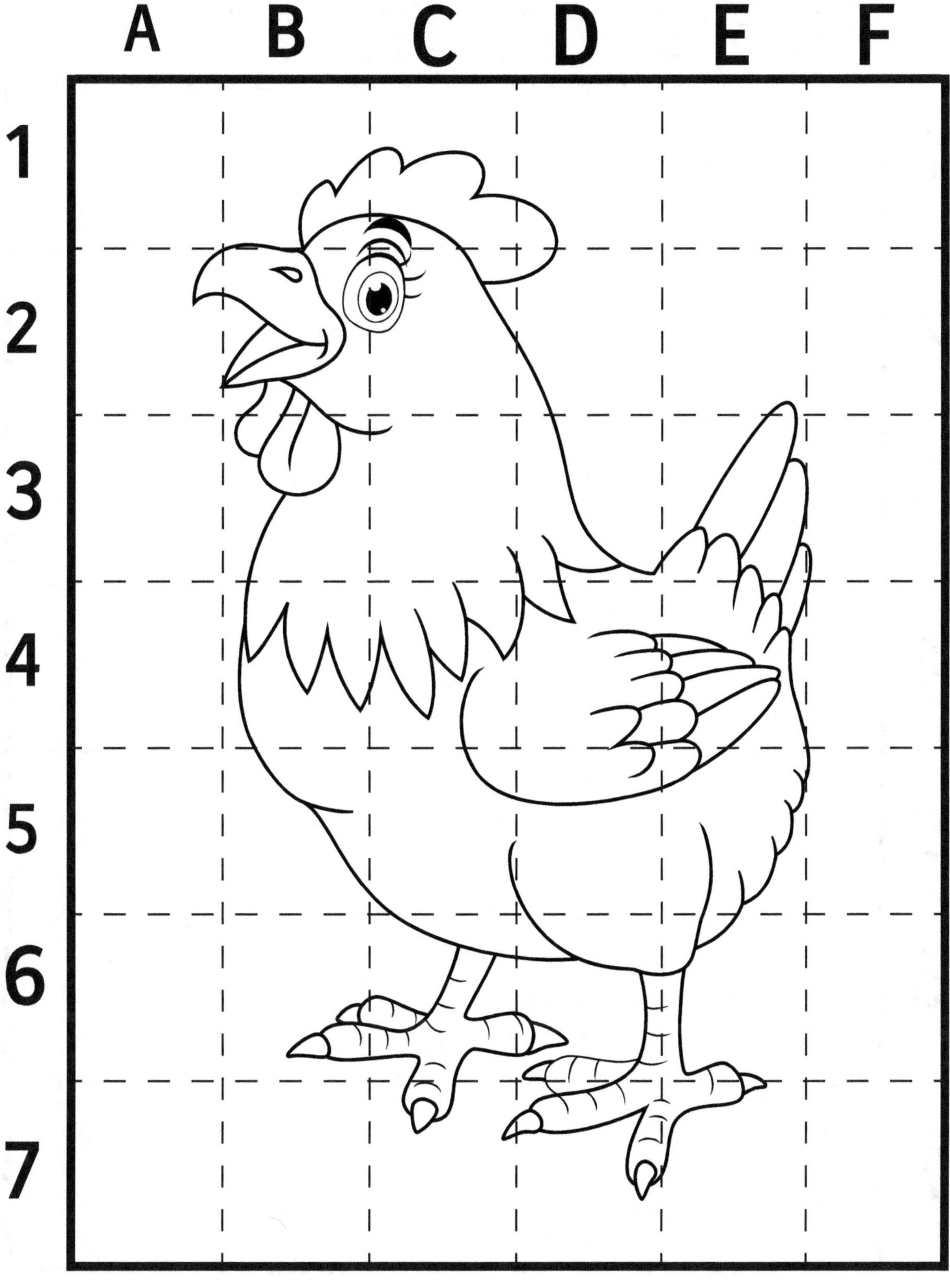

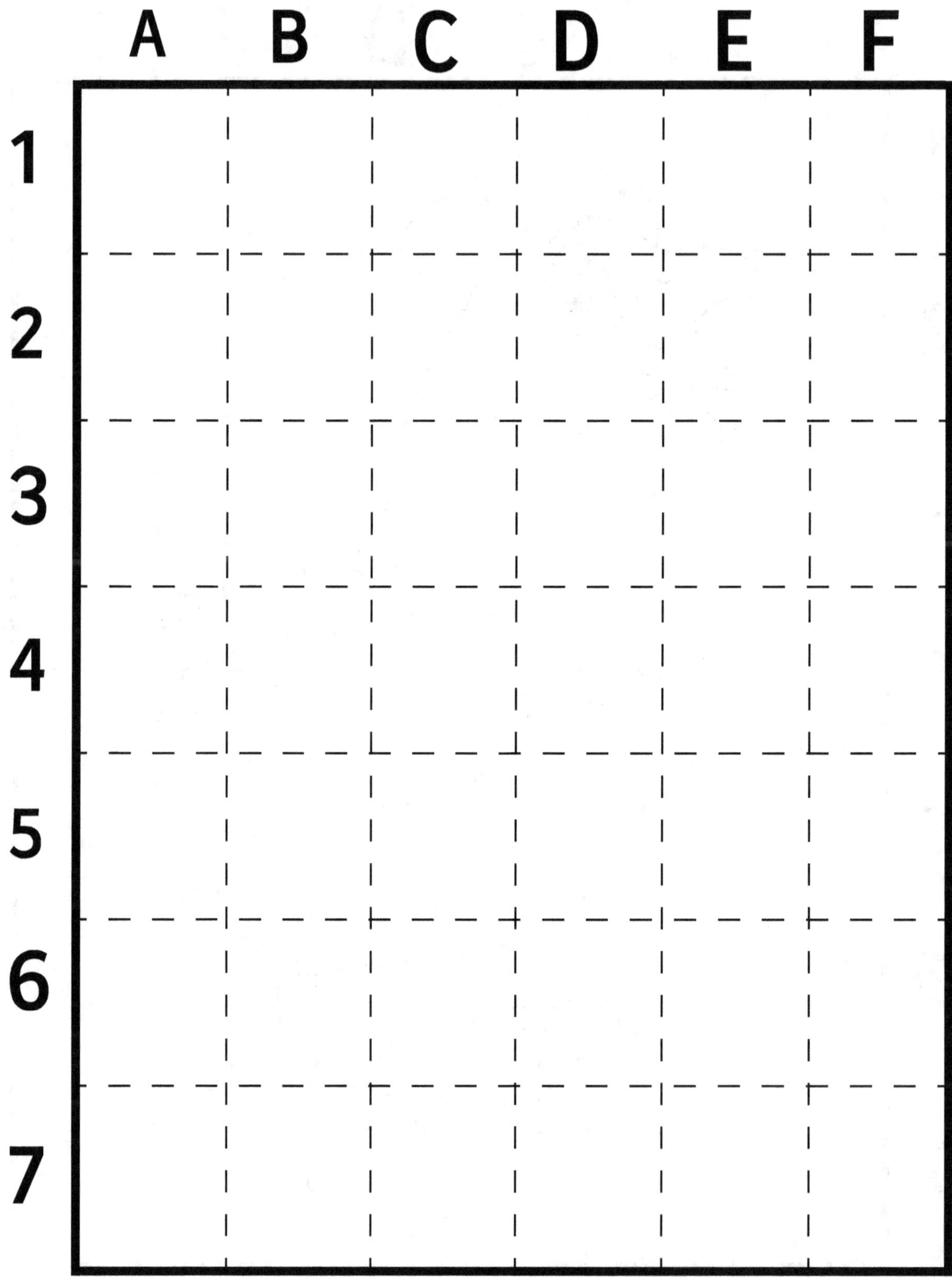

YOUR TURN!
A B C D E F
1
2
3
4
5
6
7

TRACE IT!

MAKE PARFACT

HOW TO DRAW FARM ANIMALS

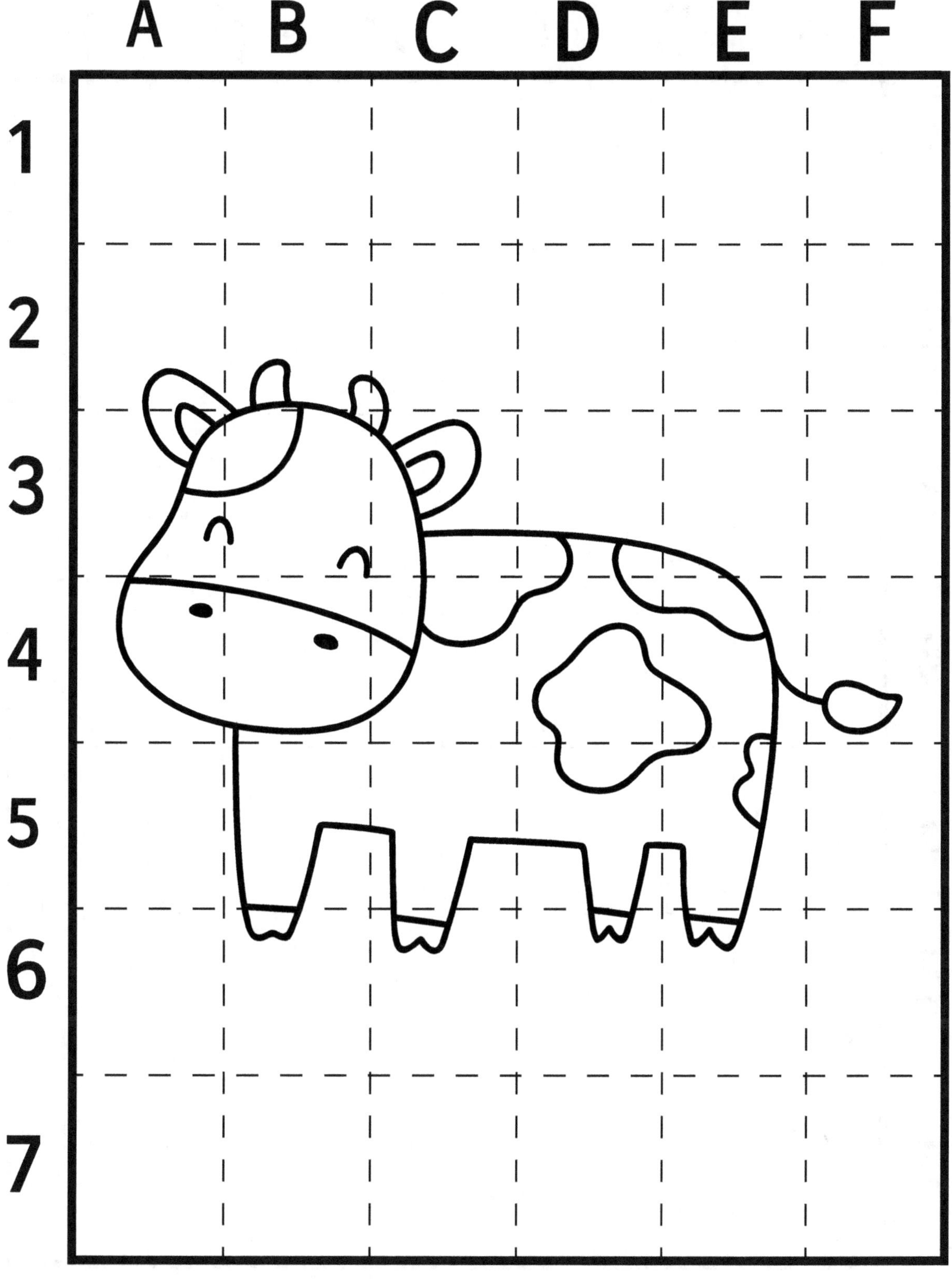

YOUR TURN!

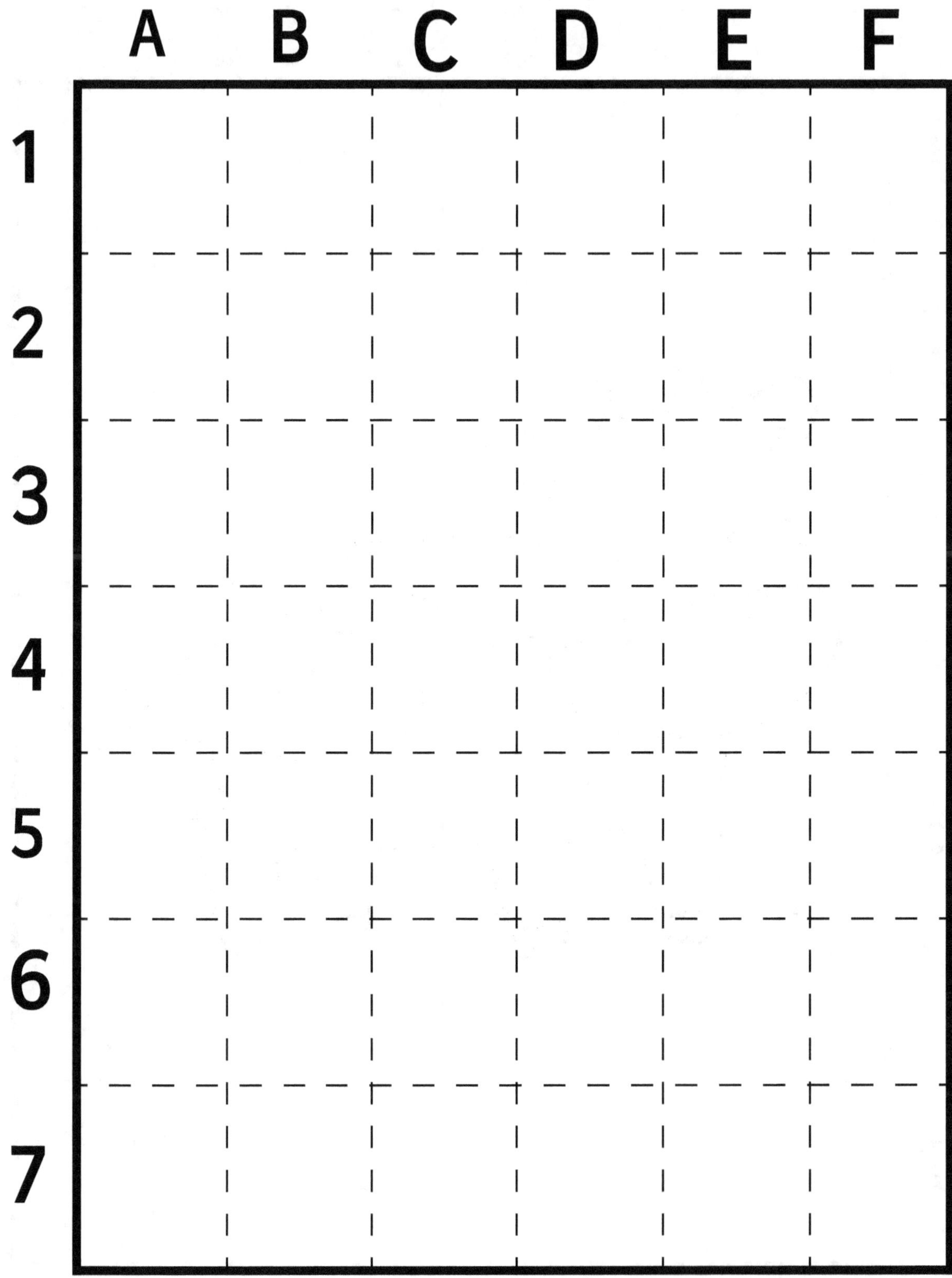

TRACE IT!

MAKE PARFACT

HOW TO DRAW FARM ANIMALS

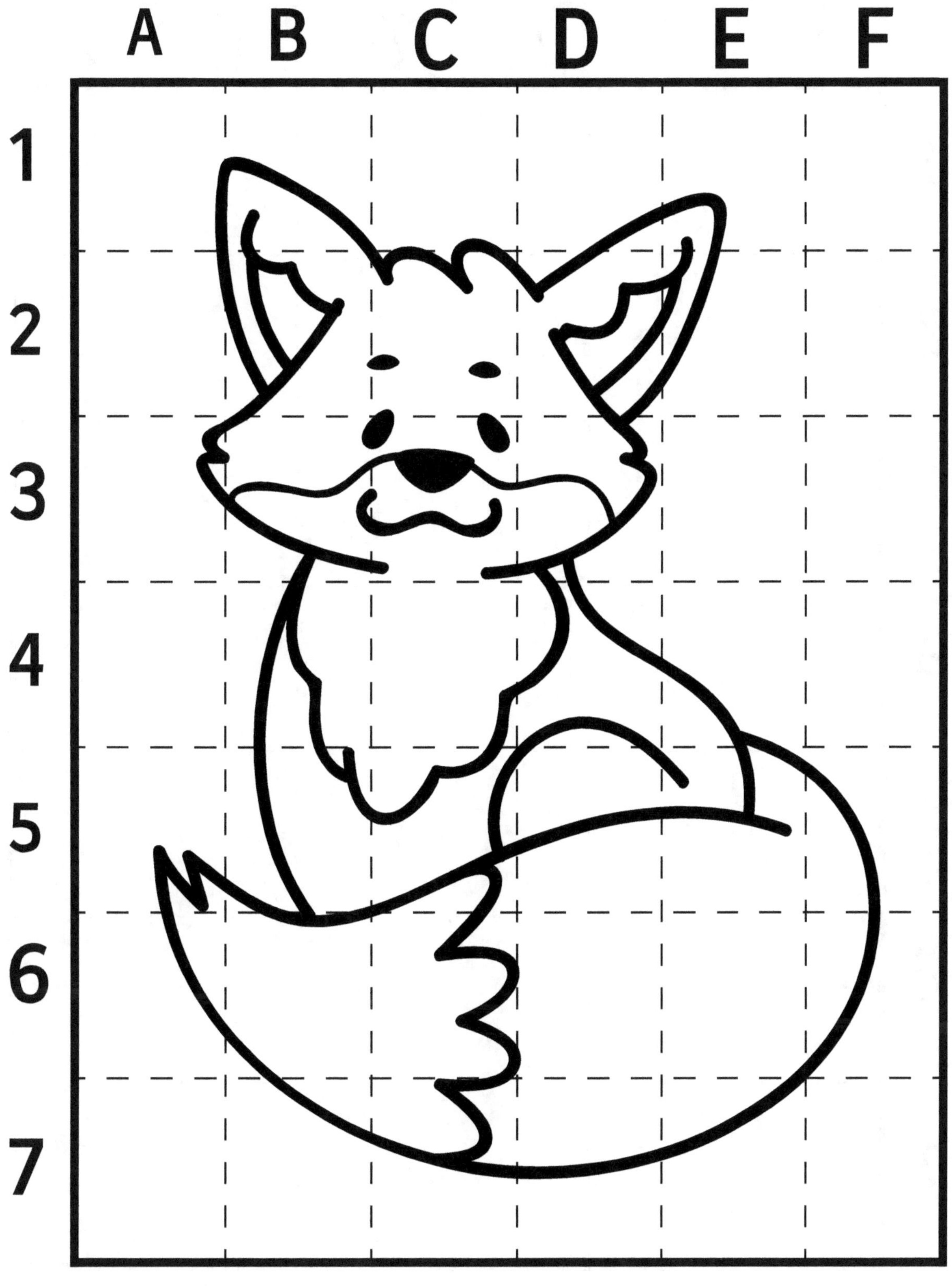

YOUR TURN!

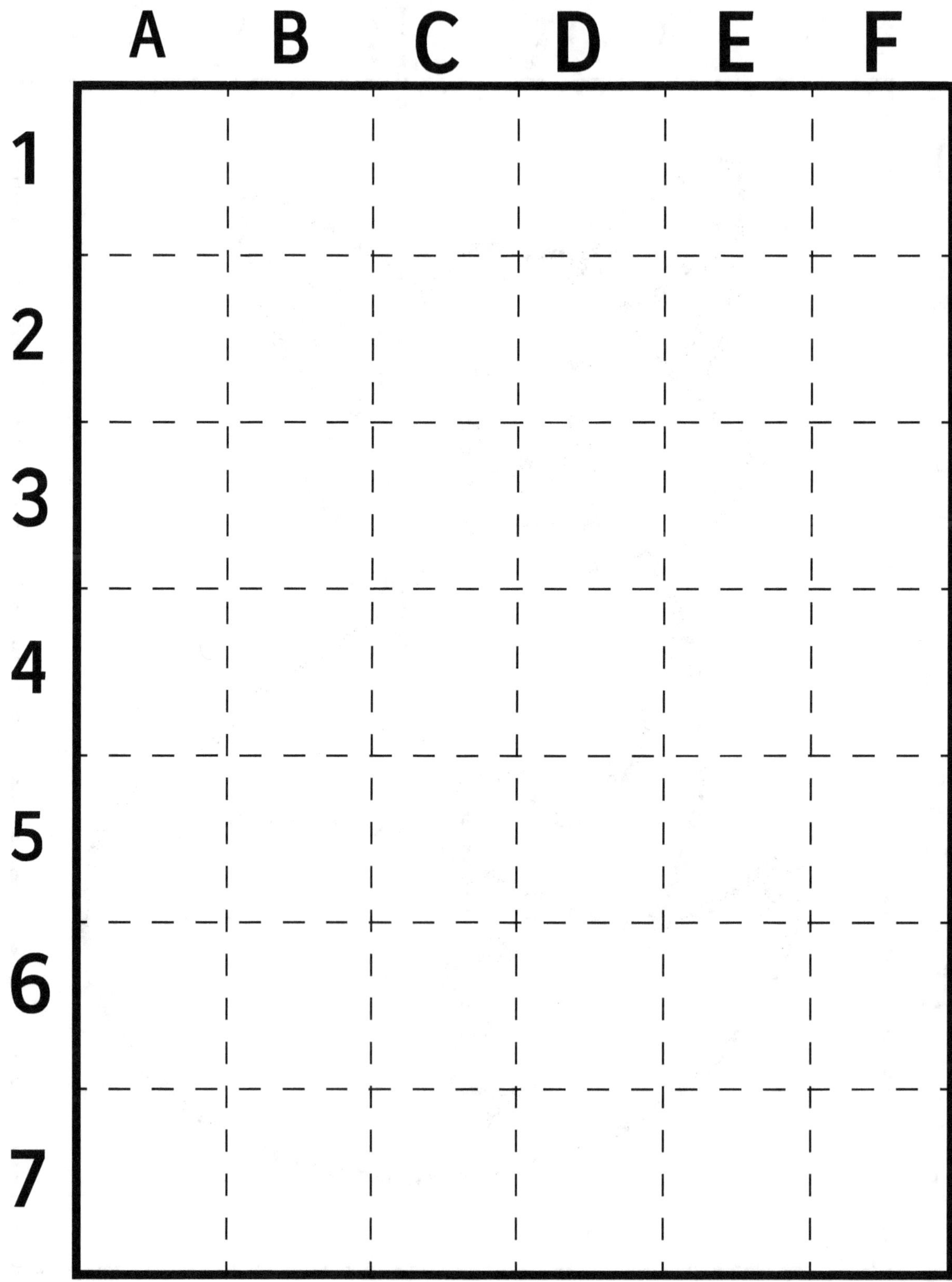

TRACE IT!

MAKE PARFACT

HOW TO DRAW FARM ANIMALS

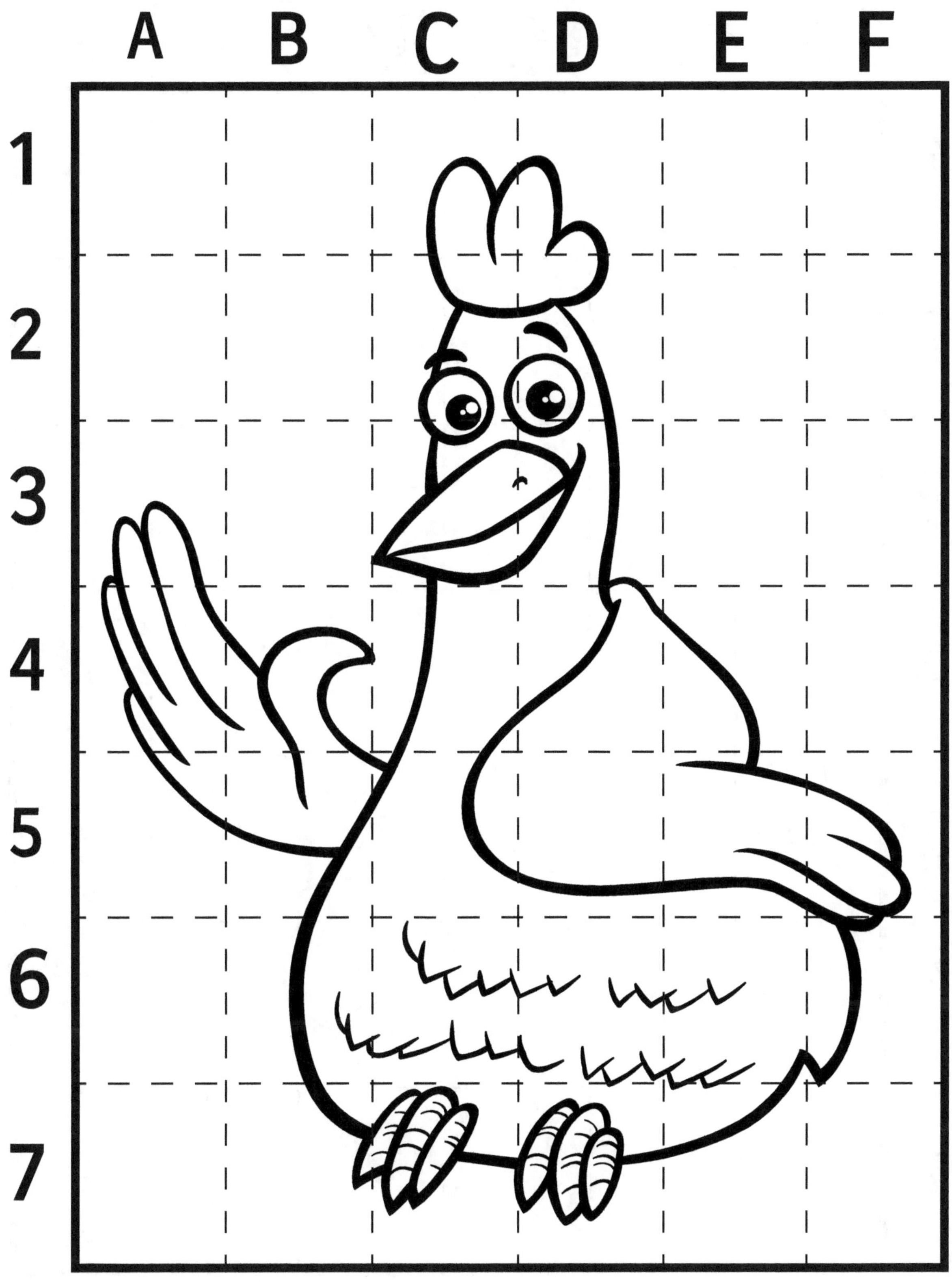

YOUR TURN!

	A	B	C	D	E	F
1						
2						
3						
4						
5						
6						
7						

TRACE IT!

MAKE PARFACT

HOW TO DRAW FARM ANIMALS

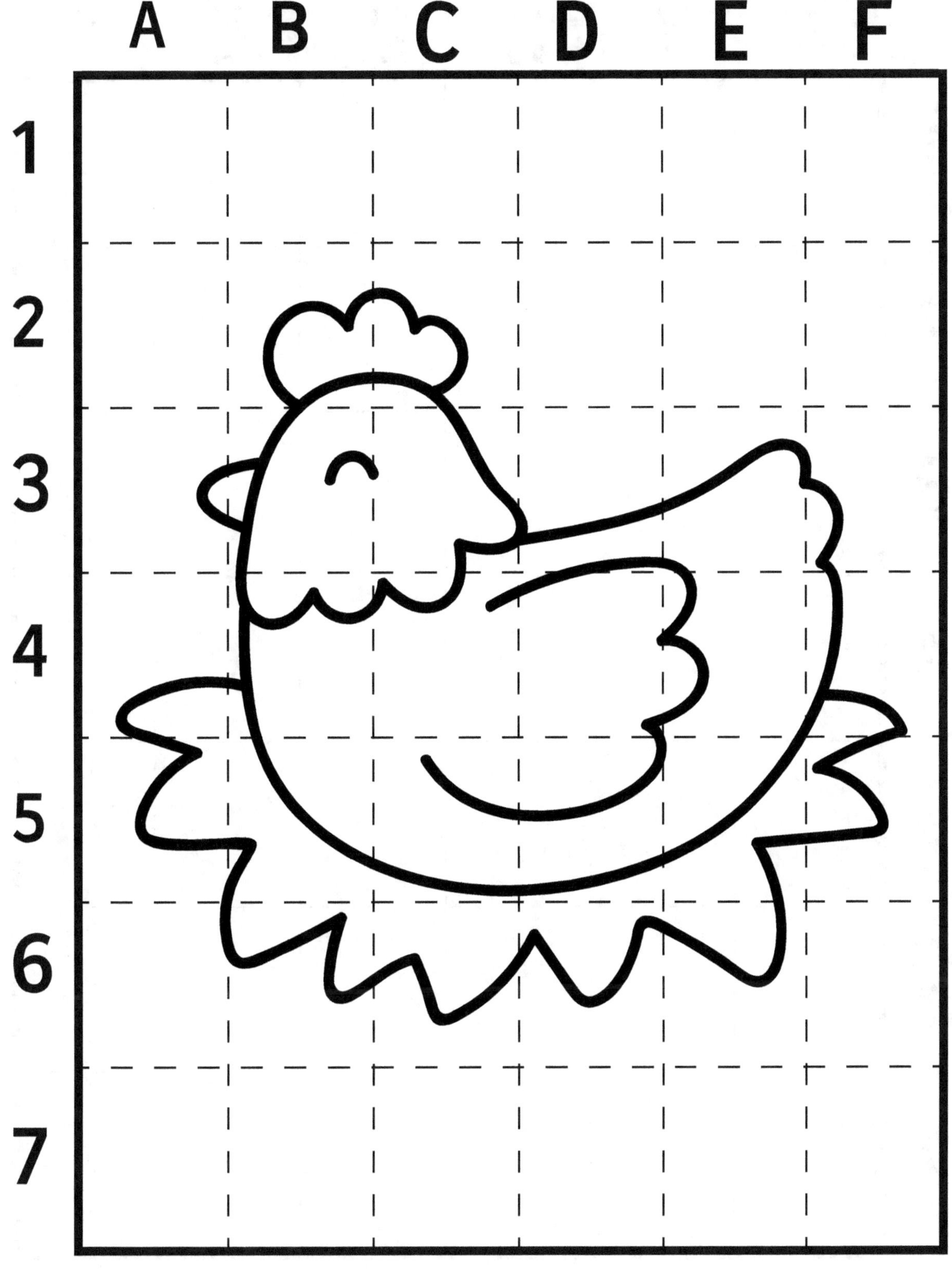

YOUR TURN!

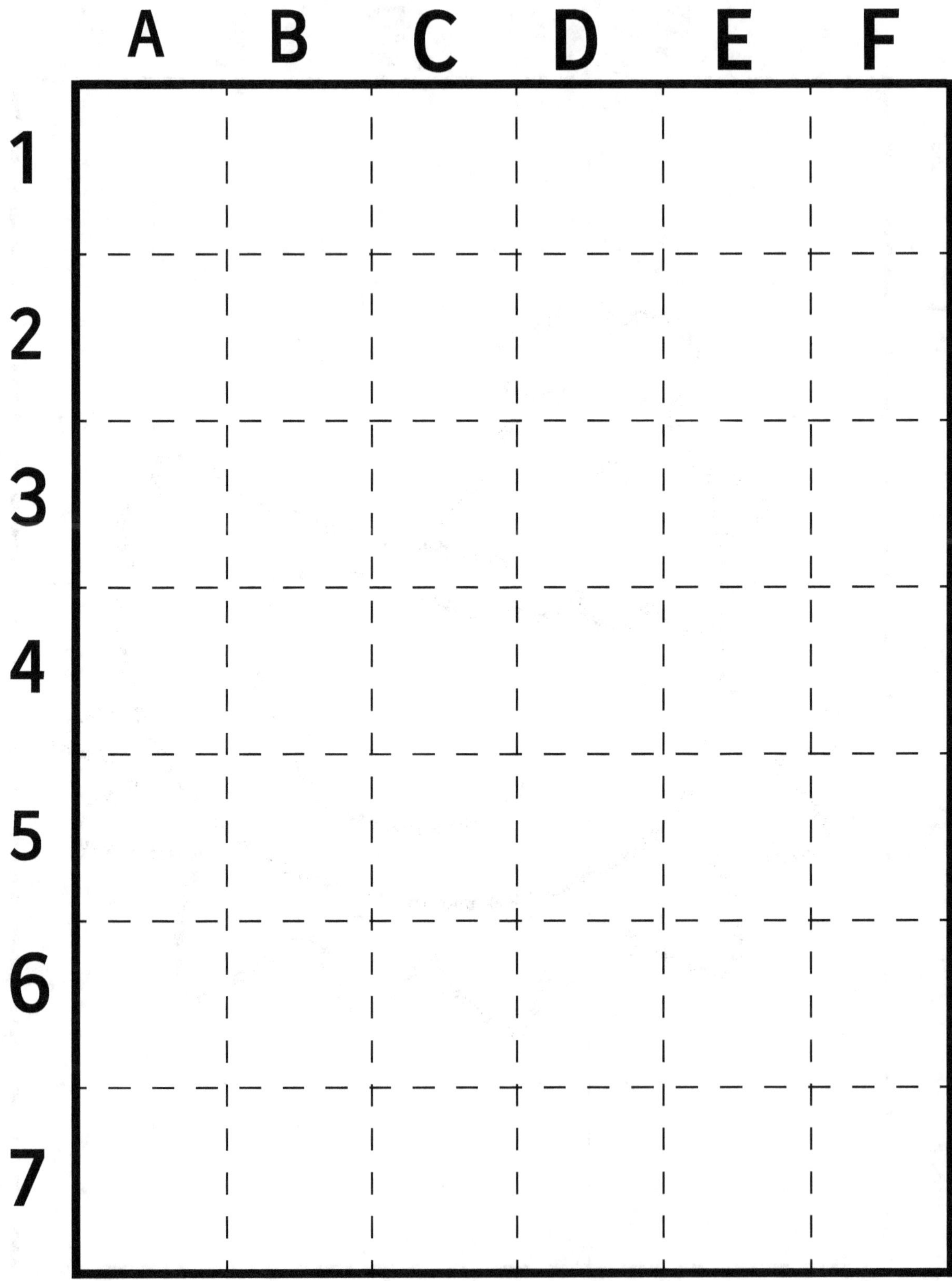

TRACE IT!

MAKE PARFACT

HOW TO DRAW FARM ANIMALS

YOUR TURN!

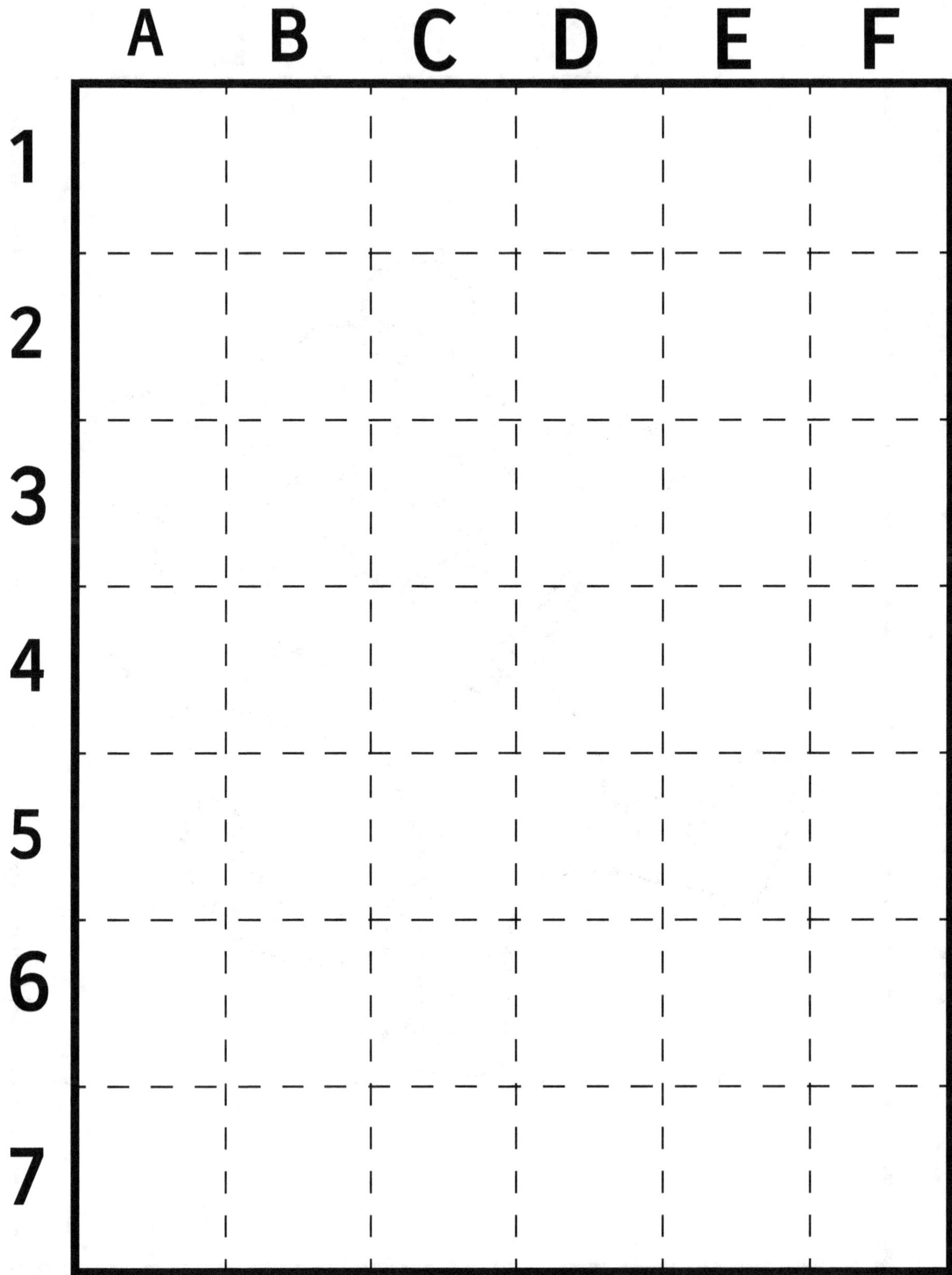

TRACE IT!

MAKE PARFACT

HOW TO DRAW FARM ANIMALS

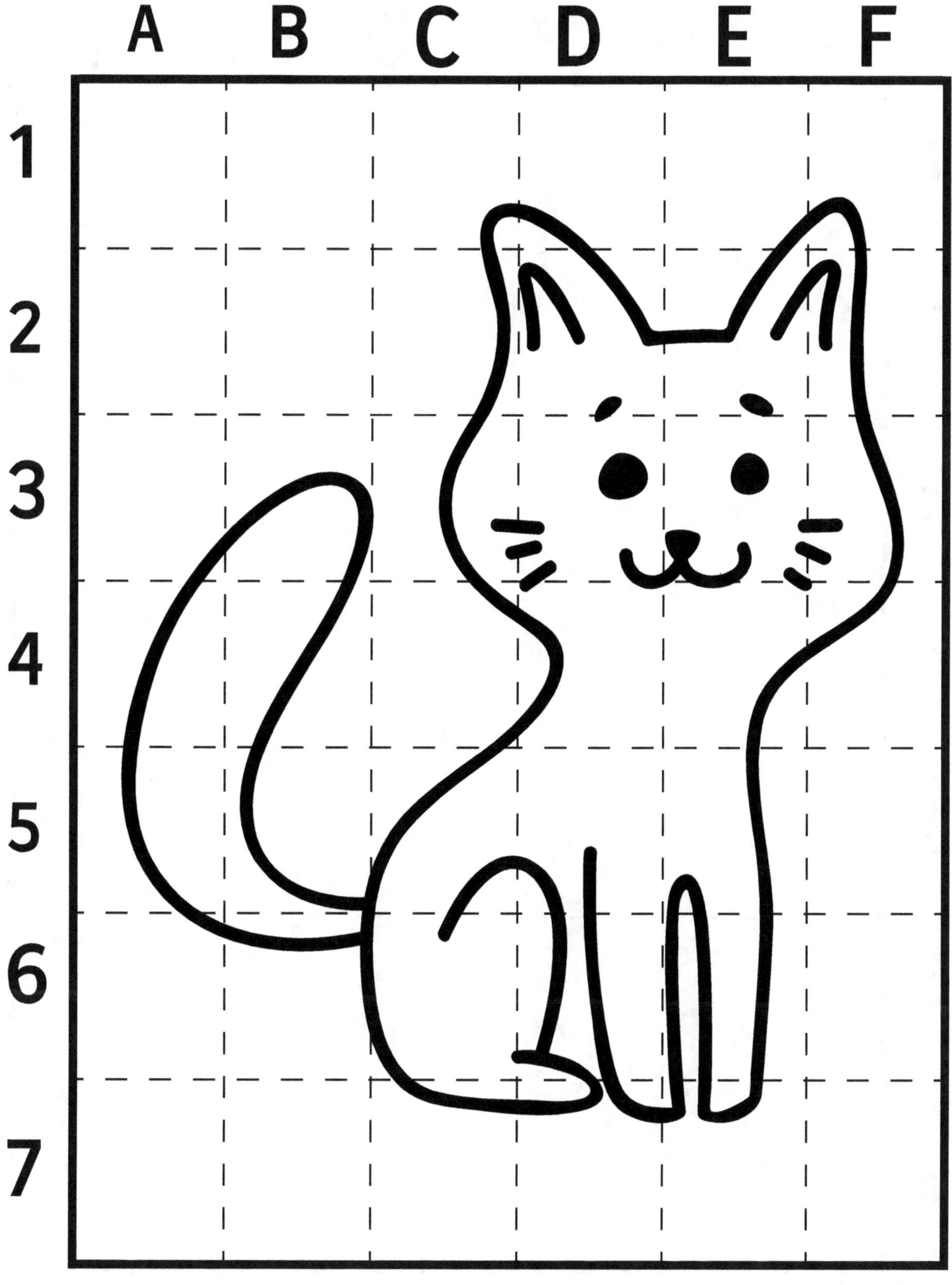

YOUR TURN!

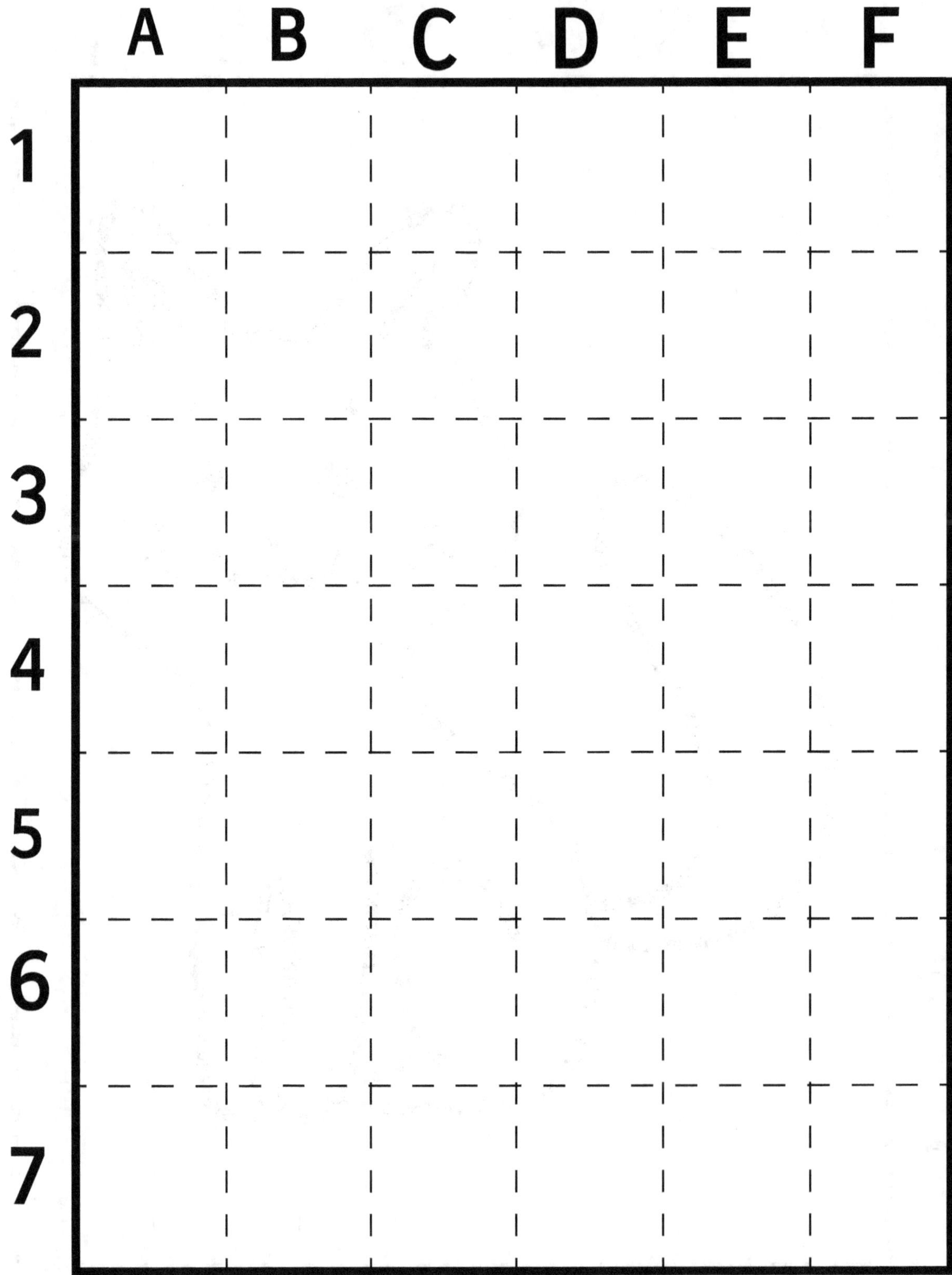

TRACE IT!

MAKE PARFACT

HOW TO DRAW FARM ANIMALS

YOUR TURN!

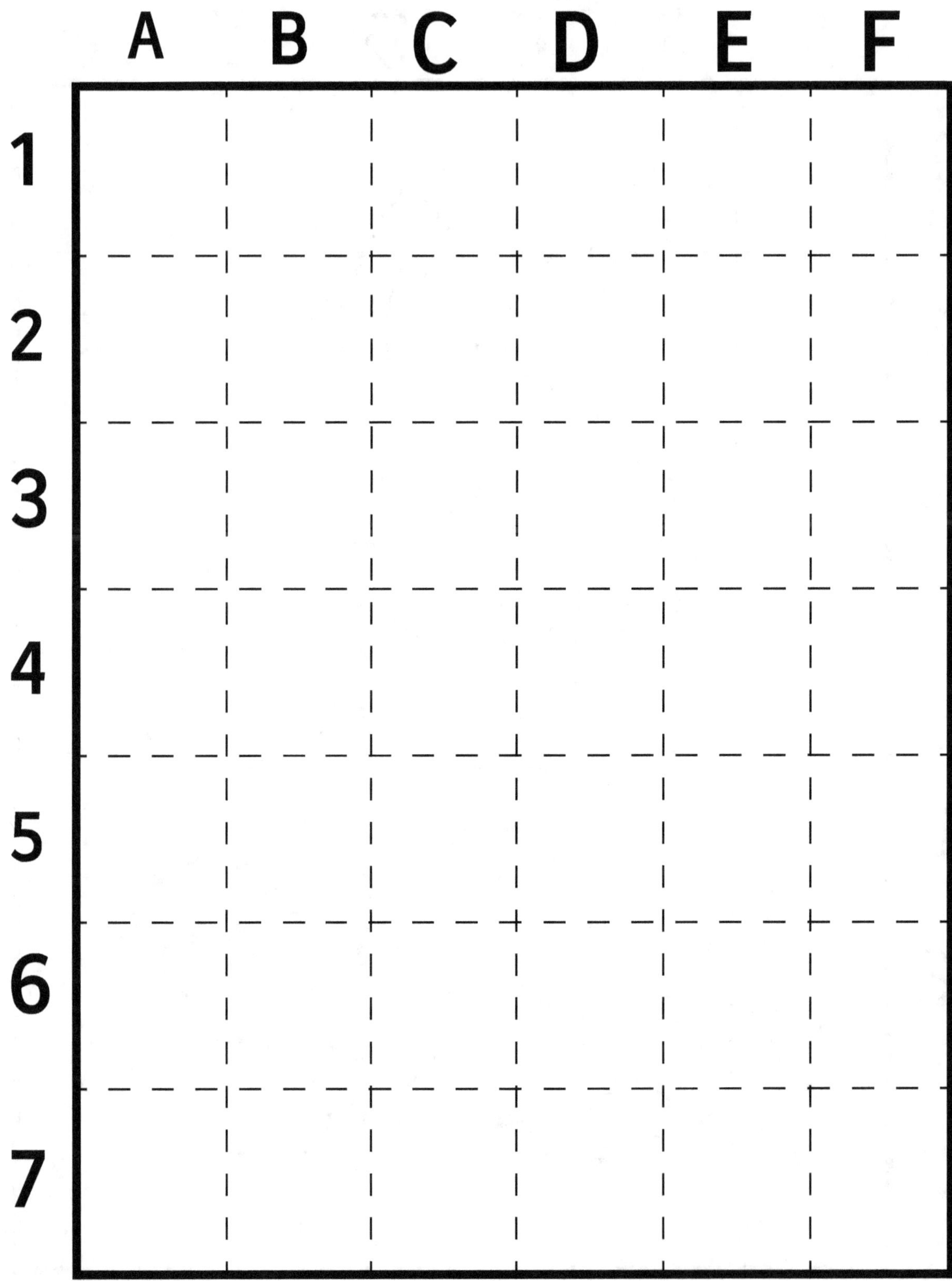

TRACE IT!

MAKE PARFACT

HOW TO DRAW FARM ANIMALS

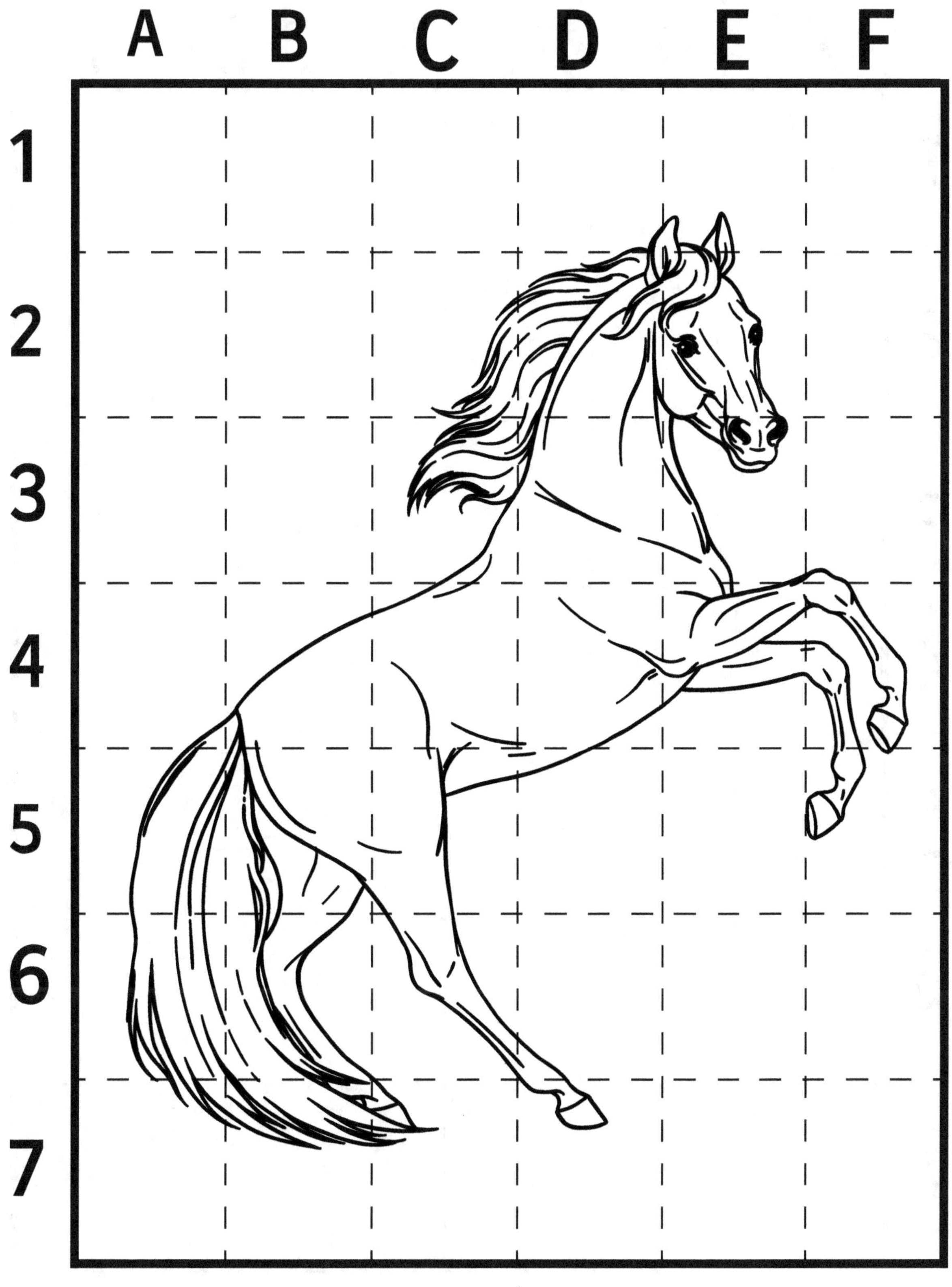

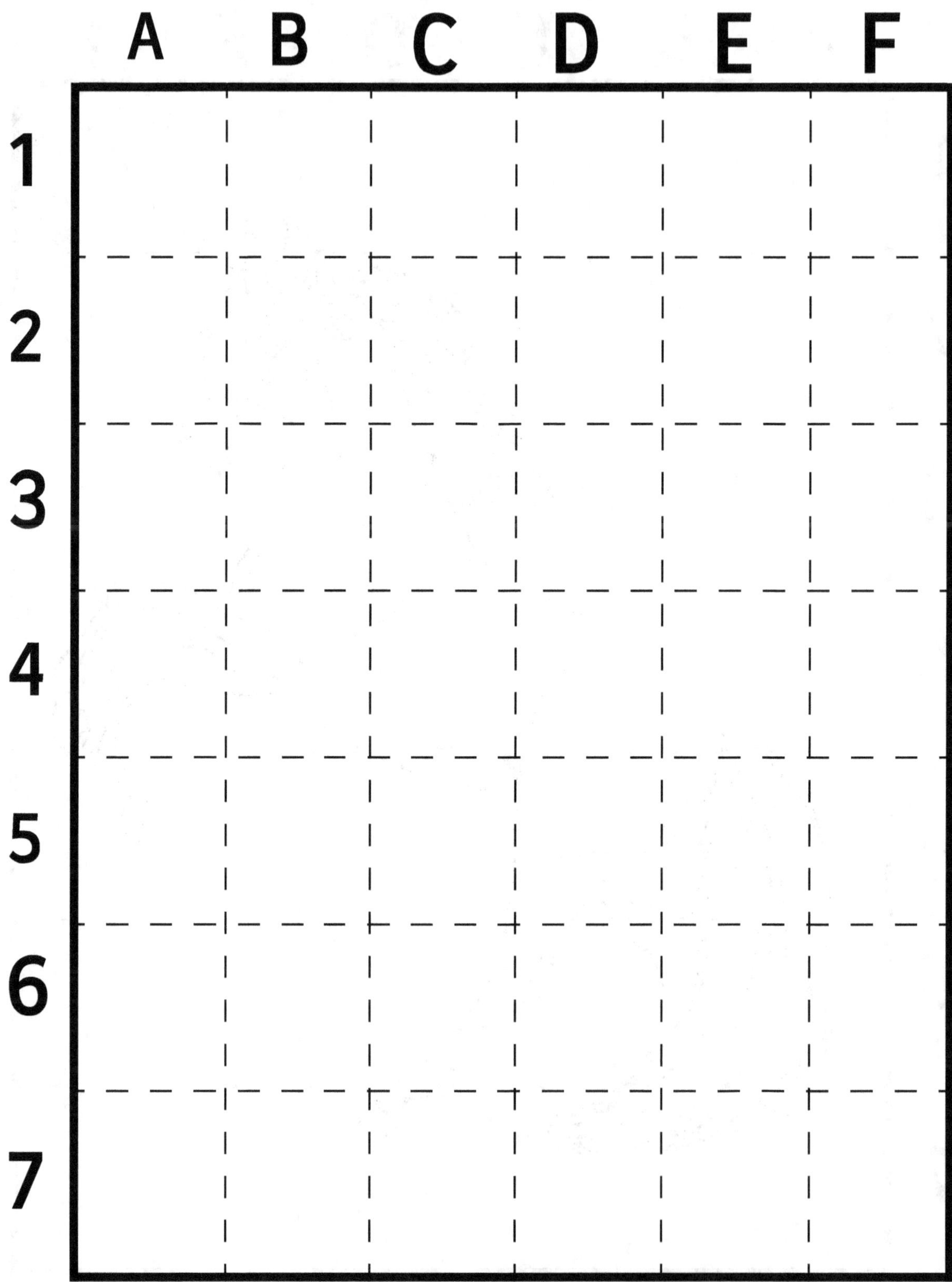

YOUR TURN!
A B C D E F
1
2
3
4
5
6
7

TRACE IT!

MAKE PARFACT

HOW TO DRAW FARM ANIMALS

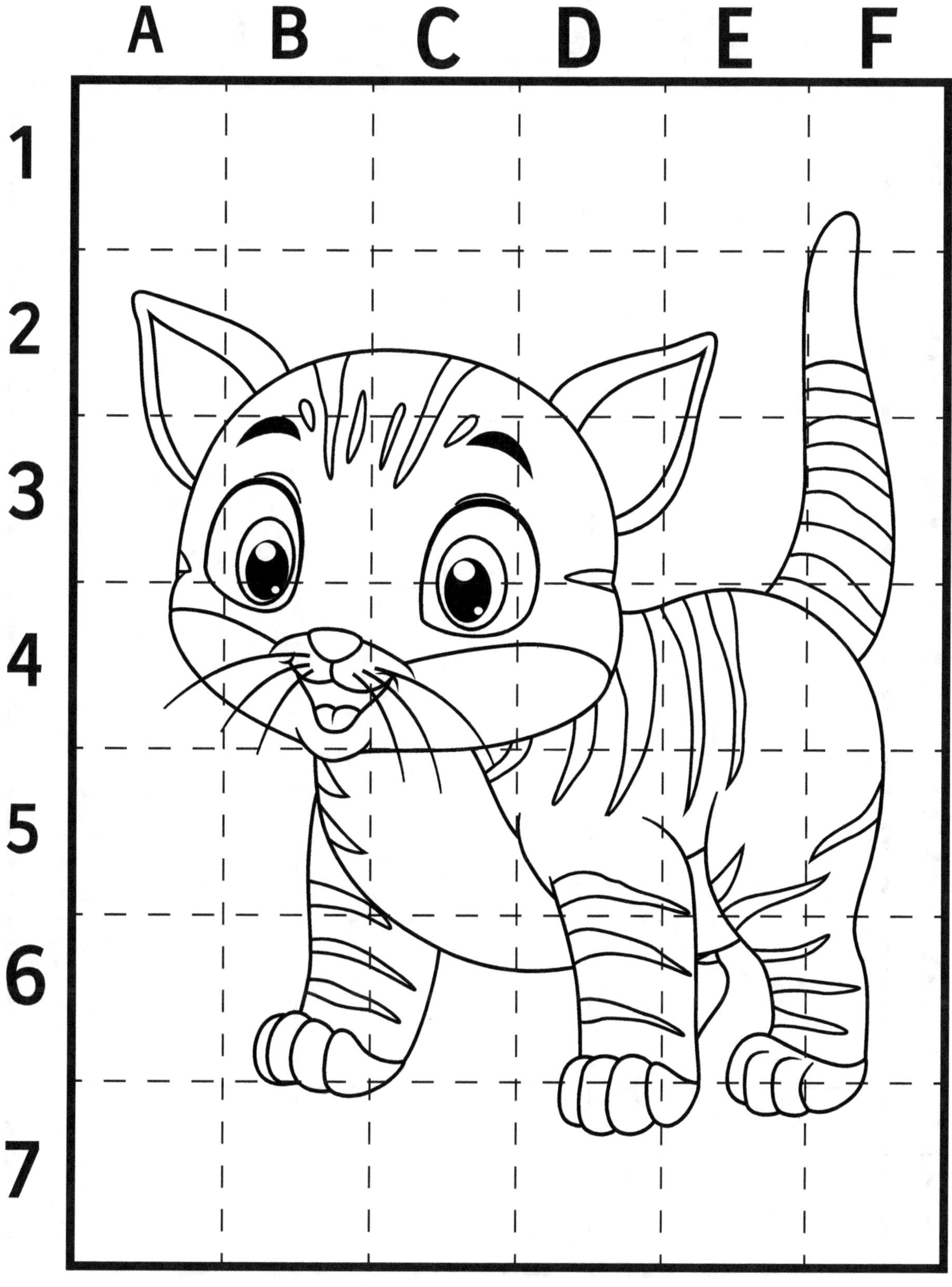

YOUR TURN!

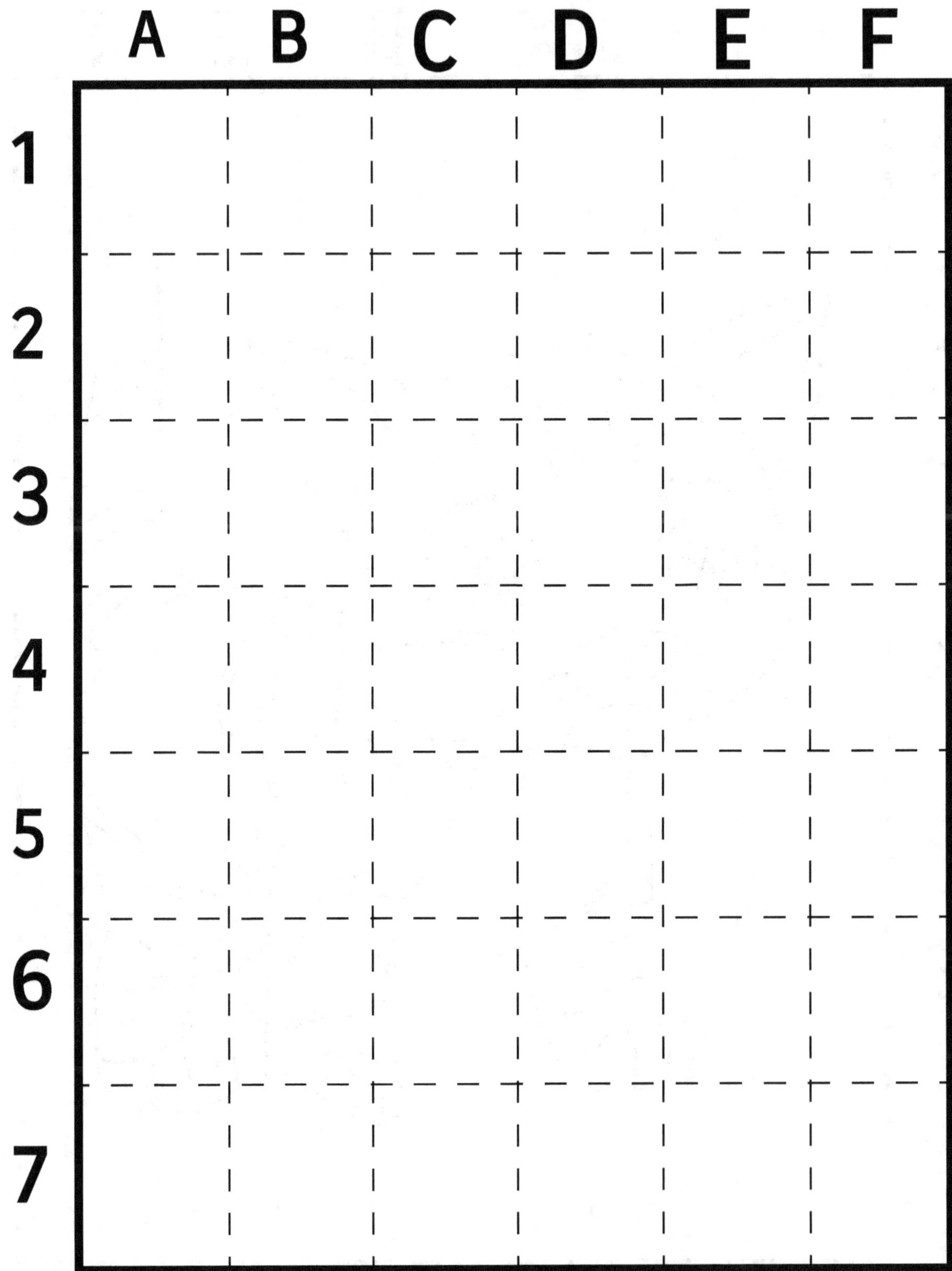

TRACE IT!

MAKE PARFACT